THE BEATLES

for Xylophone

Arrangements by Will Rapp

ISBN 978-1-70518-819-4

For all works contained herein:
Unauthorized copying, arranging, adapting, recording, internet posting, public performance,
or other distribution of the music in this publication is an infringement of copyright.
Infringers are liable under the law.

Visit Hal Leonard Online at
www.halleonard.com

World headquarters, contact:
Hal Leonard
7777 West Bluemound Road
Milwaukee, WI 53213
Email: info@halleonard.com

In Europe, contact:
Hal Leonard Europe Limited
1 Red Place
London, W1K 6PL
Email: info@halleonardeurope.com

In Australia, contact:
Hal Leonard Australia Pty. Ltd.
4 Lentara Court
Cheltenham, Victoria, 3192 Australia
Email: info@halleonard.com.au

ALL YOU NEED IS LOVE

Words and Music by JOHN LENNON
and PAUL McCARTNEY

XYLOPHONE

Copyright © 1967 Sony Music Publishing (US) LLC
Copyright Renewed
All Rights Administered by Sony Music Publishing (US) LLC, 424 Church Street, Suite 1200, Nashville, TN 37219
International Copyright Secured   All Rights Reserved

CARRY THAT WEIGHT

XYLOPHONE

Words and Music by JOHN LENNON
and PAUL McCARTNEY

Moderately

Hold 1 mallet in left, 2 mallets in right

Copyright © 1969 Sony Music Publishing (US) LLC
Copyright Renewed
All Rights Administered by Sony Music Publishing (US) LLC, 424 Church Street, Suite 1200, Nashville, TN 37219
International Copyright Secured   All Rights Reserved

HELP!

Words and Music by JOHN LENNON
and PAUL McCARTNEY

XYLOPHONE

Moderately, with a driving beat

Copyright © 1965 Sony Music Publishing (US) LLC
Copyright Renewed
All Rights Administered by Sony Music Publishing (US) LLC, 424 Church Street, Suite 1200, Nashville, TN 37219
International Copyright Secured   All Rights Reserved

A DAY IN THE LIFE

Words and Music by JOHN LENNON
and PAUL McCARTNEY

XYLOPHONE

Slowly

Copyright © 1967 Sony Music Publishing (US) LLC
Copyright Renewed
All Rights Administered by Sony Music Publishing (US) LLC, 424 Church Street, Suite 1200, Nashville, TN 37219
International Copyright Secured   All Rights Reserved

9

DO YOU WANT TO KNOW A SECRET?

Words and Music by JOHN LENNON
and PAUL McCARTNEY

XYLOPHONE

© 1963 (Renewed) NORTHERN SONGS LTD. (UK) and MPL COMMUNICATIONS, INC.
All Rights for NORTHERN SONGS LTD. (UK) in the U.S. and Canada Controlled and Administered by EMI UNART CATALOG INC. (Publishing) and ALFRED MUSIC (Print)
All Rights Reserved   Used by Permission

ELEANOR RIGBY

Words and Music by JOHN LENNON
and PAUL McCARTNEY

XYLOPHONE

Moderately

Hold 2 mallets in left, 1 mallet in right

Copyright © 1966 Sony Music Publishing (US) LLC and MPL Communications, Inc. in the United States
Copyright Renewed
All Rights for the world excluding the United States Administered by Sony Music Publishing (US) LLC, 424 Church Street, Suite 1200, Nashville, TN 37219
International Copyright Secured   All Rights Reserved

THE FOOL ON THE HILL

Words and Music by JOHN LENNON
and PAUL McCARTNEY

XYLOPHONE

Copyright © 1967 Sony Music Publishing (US) LLC
Copyright Renewed
All Rights Administered by Sony Music Publishing (US) LLC, 424 Church Street, Suite 1200, Nashville, TN 37219
International Copyright Secured   All Rights Reserved

A HARD DAY'S NIGHT

Words and Music by JOHN LENNON
and PAUL McCARTNEY

XYLOPHONE

Copyright © 1964 Sony Music Publishing (US) LLC and MPL Communications, Inc. in the United States
Copyright Renewed
All Rights for the world excluding the United States Administered by Sony Music Publishing (US) LLC, 424 Church Street, Suite 1200, Nashville, TN 37219
International Copyright Secured   All Rights Reserved

17

HELLO, GOODBYE

Words and Music by JOHN LENNON
and PAUL McCARTNEY

XYLOPHONE

Copyright © 1967 Sony Music Publishing (US) LLC
Copyright Renewed
All Rights Administered by Sony Music Publishing (US) LLC, 424 Church Street, Suite 1200, Nashville, TN 37219
International Copyright Secured   All Rights Reserved

HERE COMES THE SUN

Words and Music by
GEORGE HARRISON

XYLOPHONE

Copyright © 1969 Harrisongs Ltd.
Copyright Renewed 1998
All Rights Reserved

I SAW HER STANDING THERE

Words and Music by JOHN LENNON
and PAUL McCARTNEY

XYLOPHONE

© 1963 (Renewed) NORTHERN SONGS, LTD. and MPL COMMUNICATIONS, INC.
All Rights for NORTHERN SONGS, LTD. in the United States of America, its territories and possessions and Canada Assigned to and Controlled by
ROUND HILL WORKS on behalf of GIL MUSIC CORP.
All Rights Reserved   Used by Permission

HEY JUDE

Words and Music by JOHN LENNON
and PAUL McCARTNEY

XYLOPHONE

Copyright © 1968 Sony Music Publishing (US) LLC
Copyright Renewed
All Rights Administered by Sony Music Publishing (US) LLC, 424 Church Street, Suite 1200, Nashville, TN 37219
International Copyright Secured   All Rights Reserved

I AM THE WALRUS

Words and Music by JOHN LENNON
and PAUL McCARTNEY

XYLOPHONE

Copyright © 1967 Sony Music Publishing (US) LLC
Copyright Renewed
All Rights Administered by Sony Music Publishing (US) LLC, 424 Church Street, Suite 1200, Nashville, TN 37219
International Copyright Secured   All Rights Reserved

D.S. al Coda

CODA

Repeat and Fade

I WANT TO HOLD YOUR HAND

Words and Music by JOHN LENNON
and PAUL McCARTNEY

XYLOPHONE

Moderately

Copyright © 1963 NORTHERN SONGS LTD. and MPL COMMUNICATIONS, INC.
Copyright Renewed
All Rights for NORTHERN SONGS LTD. in the United States Administered by SONGS OF UNIVERSAL, INC.
All Rights Reserved   Used by Permission

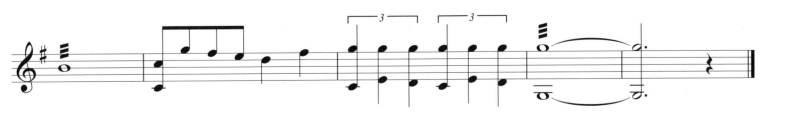

LET IT BE

Words and Music by JOHN LENNON
and PAUL McCARTNEY

XYLOPHONE

Copyright © 1970 Sony Music Publishing (US) LLC
Copyright Renewed
All Rights Administered by Sony Music Publishing (US) LLC, 424 Church Street, Suite 1200, Nashville, TN 37219
International Copyright Secured   All Rights Reserved

Guitar Solo

Vocals

rit.

THE LONG AND WINDING ROAD

Words and Music by JOHN LENNON
and PAUL McCARTNEY

XYLOPHONE

Moderately slow

Copyright © 1970 Sony Music Publishing (US) LLC
Copyright Renewed
All Rights Administered by Sony Music Publishing (US) LLC, 424 Church Street, Suite 1200, Nashville, TN 37219
International Copyright Secured   All Rights Reserved

MICHELLE

Words and Music by JOHN LENNON
and PAUL McCARTNEY

XYLOPHONE

Copyright © 1965 Sony Music Publishing (US) LLC
Copyright Renewed
All Rights Administered by Sony Music Publishing (US) LLC, 424 Church Street, Suite 1200, Nashville, TN 37219
International Copyright Secured   All Rights Reserved

PENNY LANE

Words and Music by JOHN LENNON
and PAUL McCARTNEY

XYLOPHONE

Copyright © 1967 Sony Music Publishing (US) LLC
Copyright Renewed
All Rights Administered by Sony Music Publishing (US) LLC, 424 Church Street, Suite 1200, Nashville, TN 37219
International Copyright Secured   All Rights Reserved

Opt. Bells
or single Chime tube

Straight eighth notes to end

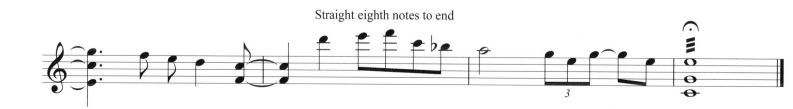

TICKET TO RIDE

Words and Music by JOHN LENNON
and PAUL McCARTNEY

XYLOPHONE

Copyright © 1965 Sony Music Publishing (US) LLC
Copyright Renewed
All Rights Administered by Sony Music Publishing (US) LLC, 424 Church Street, Suite 1200, Nashville, TN 37219
International Copyright Secured   All Rights Reserved

pp

SGT. PEPPER'S LONELY HEARTS CLUB BAND

Words and Music by JOHN LENNON
and PAUL McCARTNEY

XYLOPHONE

Moderately slow, with a steady beat

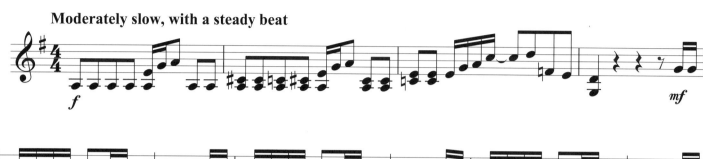

Copyright © 1967 Sony Music Publishing (US) LLC
Copyright Renewed
All Rights Administered by Sony Music Publishing (US) LLC, 424 Church Street, Suite 1200, Nashville, TN 37219
International Copyright Secured   All Rights Reserved

SHE LOVES YOU

Words and Music by JOHN LENNON
and PAUL McCARTNEY

XYLOPHONE

© 1963 (Renewed) NORTHERN SONGS, LTD. and MPL COMMUNICATIONS, INC.
All Rights for NORTHERN SONGS, LTD. in the United States of America, its territories and possessions and Canada Assigned to and Controlled by
ROUND HILL WORKS on behalf of GIL MUSIC CORP.
All Rights Reserved   Used by Permission

SOMETHING

Words and Music by
GEORGE HARRISON

XYLOPHONE

Moderately slow Ballad

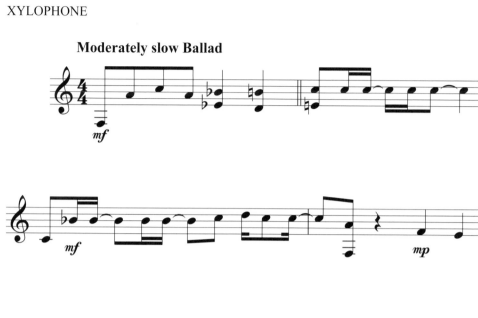

Copyright © 1969 Harrisongs Ltd.
Copyright Renewed 1998
All Rights Reserved

Bring out lower notes

WE CAN WORK IT OUT

Words and Music by JOHN LENNON
and PAUL McCARTNEY

XYLOPHONE

Copyright © 1965 Sony Music Publishing (US) LLC and MPL Communications, Inc. in the United States
Copyright Renewed
All Rights for the world excluding the United States Administered by Sony Music Publishing (US) LLC, 424 Church Street, Suite 1200, Nashville, TN 37219
International Copyright Secured   All Rights Reserved

YELLOW SUBMARINE

Words and Music by JOHN LENNON
and PAUL McCARTNEY

XYLOPHONE

Copyright © 1966 Sony Music Publishing (US) LLC and MPL Communications, Inc. in the United States
Copyright Renewed
All Rights for the world excluding the United States Administered by Sony Music Publishing (US) LLC, 424 Church Street, Suite 1200, Nashville, TN 37219
International Copyright Secured   All Rights Reserved

YESTERDAY

Words and Music by JOHN LENNON
and PAUL McCARTNEY

XYLOPHONE

Copyright © 1965 Sony Music Publishing (US) LLC and MPL Communications, Inc. in the United States
Copyright Renewed
All Rights for the world excluding the United States Administered by Sony Music Publishing (US) LLC, 424 Church Street, Suite 1200, Nashville, TN 37219
International Copyright Secured   All Rights Reserved

PURCHASE MORE GREAT BOOKS IN THE
FIRST 50 SERIES

If you've been taking music lessons for a while, you're probably eager to learn some familiar songs. These must-have collections feature well-known songs, including many instrument-specific features. These songbooks are the perfect beginning to get you playing the songs you love!

KEYBOARD INSTRUMENTS

00250269	**Accordion**	$17.99
00234685	**Electronic Keyboard** – E-Z Play Today	$18.99
00288203	**Organ**	$19.99

Dozens of piano songbooks are available in this series.
See a complete list at halleonard.com

WOODWIND INSTRUMENTS

00248843	**Flute**	$12.99
00248844	**Clarinet**	$12.99
00322933	**Bass Clarinet**	$12.99
00322934	**Bassoon**	$12.99
00322931	**Oboe**	$12.99
00248845	**Sax**	$12.99
00152493	**Harmonica**	$17.99
00282445	**Recorder**	$12.99
00322859	**Ocarina**	$12.99

BRASS INSTRUMENTS

00248846	**Trumpet**	$12.99
00322935	**Horn**	$12.99
00248847	**Trombone**	$12.99
00322937	**Tuba**	$12.99

STRING INSTRUMENTS

00248848	**Violin: Songs**	$12.99
00269155	**Violin: Classical Pieces**	$17.99
00322939	**Viola**	$12.99
00322942	**Cello**	$12.99
00252721	**Harp**	$22.99

FRETTED INSTRUMENTS

00153311	**Banjo**	$16.99
00149189	**Bass**	$16.99
00155489	**Mandolin**	$16.99
00251063	**Baritone Ukulele**	$16.99
00289029	**Solo Ukulele**	$16.99
00292982	**Ukulele Melodies**	$16.99
00149250	**Ukulele Songs**	$19.99

Dozens of guitar songbooks are available in this series.
See a complete list at halleonard.com

DRUM/PERCUSSION

00175795	**Drums**	$17.99
00322944	**Bells/Glockenspiel**	$12.99
00294919	**Marimba**	$14.99
00276997	**Snare Drum**	$16.99
00299648	**Vibraphone**	$15.99
00320031	**Xylophone**	$15.99

VOCALS

00196404	**Broadway Songs** – High Voice	$16.99
00196405	**Broadway Songs** – Low Voice	$16.99

RECORDING

00294443	**Recording Techniques to Track Music**	$15.99

View complete songlists and more songbooks
at www.halleonard.com

HAL•LEONARD®

Prices, contents and availability
subject to change without notice.
All prices listed in U.S. funds.

235
0623